The Man Who

A Theatrical Research

Peter Brook

and

Marie-Hélène Estienne

Methuen Drama

Methuen Drama

3 5 7 9 10 8 6 4 2

Published in Great Britain in 2002 by
Methuen Publishing Limited

Inspired by *The Man who Mistook
his Wife for a Hat* by Oliver Sacks
(Peter Smith Publishers, New York, 1992)

Copyright © 2002 Peter Brook and Marie-Hélène Estienne

The authors have asserted their moral rights

A CIP catalogue record for this book is available
from the British Library

ISBN 0 413 77141 5

Typeset by SX Composing DTP, Rayleigh, Essex
Printed and bound in Great Britain by
Cox and Wyman Ltd, Reading, Berkshire

Preface

If a man mistakes his wife for a hat, there must be a reason. Is he mad? The moment we lay aside this easy assumption, we face a real mystery.

For it is not only the title that has turned Oliver Sacks' book into a bestseller: behind it lies an unknown world in which each new discovery we make is both fascinating and deeply moving.

Sacks is a neurologist – a 'romantic neurologist', as he says himself – for whom the most essential clinical instrument is his own heart, as it once was for another doctor, Anton Chekhov, who observed the vagaries of the human soul with equal compassion. For Sacks, those who suffer from the hardest and most painful complaints are not diminished human beings: they are warriors struggling across inner chasms and abysses with the courage and determination of tragic heroes.

For a long while, within our theatre work, I have been searching for a common ground that could involve the spectator directly, without the need to rely on pictures from the past, nor on the over-familiar images of the present. Today the great new subject of universal interest is the brain and we do not need to look far to discover why. Whatever the social and national barriers, we all have a brain and we think we know it. But the moment we go inside, we find we are on another planet. In the words of the Persian poem 'The Conference of the Birds', 'this is the valley of astonishment'.

As we began to work, we felt the need to experience this astonishment at first hand. Thanks to Sacks' inspiration we observed cases like the ones he described, similar yet different.

They became a starting point in our search for a theatre form.

Peter Brook

The Man Who was first performed, in English, at the Theaterhaus Gessnerallee, Zurich, Switzerland, on 18 February 1994. The cast was as follows:

David Bennent
Sotigui Kouyate
Bruce Myers
Yoshi Oida

Directed by Peter Brook
Music by Mahmoud Tabrizi-Zadeh

Stimuli

*The **Doctor** touches the right side of the **Patient**'s head with an electrode. The **Patient**'s hand moves slightly. The **Doctor** changes the places of the electrode, always on the right side. The **Patient** reacts to the different stimuli with a series of movements. Then the **Doctor** puts the electrode on the left side.*

Patient   I smell the earth. I'm coming back from school, with my brothers. We are walking in a field. There's a man in front of us, carrying a sack. He says, 'Do you want to climb in?' It's full of snakes. I'm very frightened. My brothers are shouting 'Go away! Go away! Run!' I am in my village Baouega.

*The **Doctor** removes the electrode, then puts it back in the same place.*

Patient   I've just told you it's Baouega.

*The **Doctor** takes away the electrode.*

Patient   Please, doctor, again . . .

*The **Doctor** puts it back again, but this time on another place.*

Patient   No, it's not Baouega. It's Nekrou. My father is there. He says, 'The morning is over, the afternoon has gone by and night is still to come. The house was built and will be destroyed, we will build another and it too will be destroyed . . .'

*The **Patient** begins to have an epileptic fit. The **Doctor** runs to help him. He calms down and turns to them.*

Patient   It's strange, I was there and here at the same time.

Frontal Lobe 1

A **Patient** *is sitting at a table, staring fixedly at an unlit candle. He takes a match from a box beside him, lights it, blows it out. He is about to light it again when the* **Doctor** *who has been observing him puts his hand on his arm.*

Doctor   If you please, don't light the candle.

Patient   Very well.

The **Doctor** *takes away the matches.*

Doctor   Do you know where you are?

Patient   In hospital.

Doctor   You know why you are in hospital?

Patient   Yes, my son had an accident.

Doctor   Your son?

Patient   Yes.

The **Doctor** *places the matches close to the* **Patient**.

Doctor   Wasn't it you I examined yesterday?

Patient   Yes, you fiddled with my ear. I feel much better now. Thank you.

The **Patient** *lights a match and moves it towards the candle.*

Doctor   Didn't I ask you not to light the candle?

Patient   Excuse me. (*He blows out the match.*)

Doctor   I'm going to tap twice on the table, like this.

He does so. The **Patient** *at once begins to copy him.*

Doctor   Wait. I'll tap twice and you once. Yes?

Patient   Yes.

Doctor   I tap twice, you once.

Patient   Once, yes. (*He taps twice.*)

Doctor   Very well. Since you prefer tapping twice, you'll go on tapping twice and I'll tap once. Clear?

Patient   Quite clear!

*The **Doctor** taps once. The **Patient** also taps once. The **Doctor** makes various gestures: crosses his arms, his legs, stands. The **Patient** does likewise. The **Doctor** puts his hands together in prayer. The **Patient** does likewise.*

Doctor   Now tell me, why have you put your hands together like this?

Patient   Because you asked me to.

Doctor   I never asked you anything.

Patient   But you did it.

Doctor   Yes, but I've never asked you to do what I did.

Patient   But since you did it, it was obvious.

Frontal Lobe 2

A **Patient** *is waiting.*

Doctor   Sit down. If I'm not mistaken, you were a teacher in a religious institution.

Patient   Yes.

Doctor   What were you teaching in this institution?

Patient   Psycho-physio.

Doctor   Spiritual psycho-physio?

Patient   Yes.

Doctor   Then you must know what the Vatican is.

Patient   The Vatican, yes.

Doctor   What is the Vatican?

Patient   In principle, it's an oral demonstration, eventually an Aboriginal Africa quite simply. Pope John the Twenty-Second lives there, around him there are the other popes: John Twenty-Two, John Twenty-Three, John Twenty-Four, John Twenty-Five, John Twenty-Six, and the archangels as well.

Doctor   Where is the Vatican?

Patient   In the city of Rome in Spain.

Doctor   What's the Pope's nationality?

Patient   He is Spanish from New Zealand.

Doctor   Tell me some names of animals.

Patient   A monkey, an elephant, a Buffalo Bill, a tickle my foot, a giraffe, an ass's back, a zigomat, a buffalo, two buffaloes, three buffaloes, four buffaloes, five buffaloes, six buffaloes, seven buffaloes, eight buffaloes, nine buffaloes . . .

Doctor   Good. Now some words beginning with the letter F.

Patient   A fact, a fetish, a factotum, a fiasco, a fabrication, a phenomenon, a two times twenty, a fippopotamus, a frigoïd.

Doctor   What day is it today?

Patient   Paedophilia.

The **Doctor** *shows him a pen.*

Doctor   What's this?

Patient   A mystical ambulance.

The **Doctor** *shows him a red pen.*

Doctor   And this?

Patient   A red mystical ambulance.

Doctor   Describe me a drum.

Patient   Ah, that's not so easy. It's a resonating instrument that's round. It rocks. You can unwind the drum, the cables, its body's like a crooked woman, with a belt in the middle. And it's covered with parchment, in front, behind and on the sides.

Doctor   If I say 'Little Red Riding Hood', what does that mean to you?

Patient   A caretaker with ten keys.

Doctor   Perhaps you know her story? Can you tell it to me?

Patient   A hunter in a forest with his wife. There's a little girl dressed in red. They make her a little red hood. She's very pretty. The colour attracts him. She begins to run, the wolf runs as well, so as to catch her and chew her up. Perhaps that's not quite right.

Doctor   Very good. Now we'll try something harder. Take these three words: crisis, minister, president. Now make up a sentence with these three words.

Patient   The president asked the kitchen to boil him an egg.

Doctor   And a sentence with crowd and heap.

Patient   A heap is a badly made crowd. Anyone can get into it. Nobody worth anything would ever be in a heap.

Doctor   Absolutely true! Let's try something different . . . Please draw a large circle on the table.

He gives a felt pen to the **Patient***, who slowly and laboriously draws a circle on a large sheet of paper. However, when it is complete, he cannot stop. The movement of his arm gets faster and faster. The circle becomes a frenetic spiral, until it reaches a central point where the hand cannot stop rotating obsessively. The* **Doctor** *gently checks the movement.*

Doctor   Thank you. It's very beautiful.

Autist

A **Doctor** *is putting some plastic cubes on a table. A* **Patient** *enters, goes towards the cubes and studies them intensely.* **Doctor 2** *is present.*

Doctor   Tell me, what have you been doing this morning?

Autist   I got up at 8.46. I had a shower, which took 12 minutes, 18 seconds. Then I had breakfast. As there were clouds and a little sun, I only half-filled my glass of orange juice. If there'd been bright sun, I'd've been able to fill it to the brim. I ate 3 slices of bread and butter and as I am 12 years old I ate 12 raisins.
You, how many raisins do you eat?

Doctor   165.

Autist   Then he's 165 years old.

Doctor 2   Perhaps.

Autist   Next, I went down the 92 steps of my house. I passed 9 street lamps on the way to the baker's, and in front of your house I tapped 3 times on each of the 3 iron bars of your railing. I came in, you were late, I waited for 37 minutes, 49 seconds, next to your secretary, who can type 110 words in 3 minutes, which makes 6 point 1,1,1,1,1 to infinity, then I came in here. (*He points at one* **Doctor***, then at the other.*) You have 4 pens in your pocket, you have 1 and now I'm off, going to the door in 27 steps.

The **Doctor** *catches his arm to restrain him. The* **Autist** *lets out a howl of pain. Then he takes the* **Doctor***'s hand, very gently scoops an imaginary lump of flesh from the palm and, with the greatest care, replaces it on the part of his arm that the* **Doctor** *had held. The* **Doctor** *now indicates the table.*

Doctor   Good. Wait. Watch carefully. (*He covers a small blue box with one of the plastic cubes.*) If I ask the doctor 'Where is the little blue box?' what will he say?

Autist   It's there.

Doctor Why?

Autist Because he put it there. I saw him.

Doctor Good. Leave us, doctor.

*The **Second Doctor** leaves. The **First Doctor** conspiratorially takes the blue box from under the cube and hides it under another cube.*

Doctor Come back, doctor. Now, if I ask the doctor 'Where is the little blue box?' what will he say?

Autist It's there.

*Without hesitation, the **Autist** points to the new hiding place.*
***Doctor 2** points to the cube where it was first hidden.*

Doctor 2 When I left, it was there.

*The **Autist** shakes his head, indicating the other cube.*

Autist He put it there. I saw him.

Doctor 2 But I was not here. I didn't see it.

Autist So what?

He goes out, counting his steps: '1,2,3,4,5,6,7 . . .'

The Man from La Rochelle

Doctor   Good morning.

Patient   Good morning.

Doctor   Sit down.
Every time I raise my right hand, say 'La Rochelle'.

He does so.

Patient   La Rochelle . . .

The **Doctor** *waits. The* **Patient** *repeats, with slightly less conviction . . .*

Patient   La Rochelle.

The **Doctor** *waits a little longer, raises his hand.*

Patient   La R . . .

The **Doctor** *waits, raises his hand again. The* **Patient** *remains silent, without movement.*

Doctor   Tell me, where are we now? In what town?

Patient   Paris.

Doctor   No. You've been here for 27 years and you don't know where you are?

Patient   27 years? I just got here this morning.

Doctor   Where?

Patient   Here. Paris.

Doctor   But we're in La Rochelle.

Patient   Are you sure? Well . . .

Doctor   Do you know La Rochelle?

Patient   Yes, I went there once.

Doctor   What for?

Patient   For a bit of fresh air. Well not exactly . . .
I went to see someone I knew, a young lady, it's like this. I
took the train to La Rochelle. I went to 27 rue des Voiliers –
that's where she lived – I saw her, we made love, it wasn't
any better or worse than with the others, and then I came
back to Paris.

Doctor   Did you see anything interesting in La Rochelle?

Patient   Nothing at all.

Doctor   Did you see the sea?

Patient   No, I've never seen the sea. But I'd like to, very
much. It must be very beautiful.

Doctor   Do you drink?

Patient   A little glass from time to time, after all, if you
can't have a drop with your friends from time to time,
what's the use of living? I mean . . . after all . . .

Doctor   Listen carefully. I'm going to give you a sentence
and you'll try to repeat it. Yesterday, I met a bear who was
riding a bicycle.

Patient   Not true! After all, why not? In a circus bears
ride bicycles. Yesterday, there was a big circus near the
church with lots of animals, not far from the church, over
there, the day before yesterday, no yesterday.

Doctor   What's the sentence?

Patient   Yesterday I went to the church, I saw a bear
who'd climbed on top of the other animals, something like
that, who was telling the other animals what to do.

Doctor   No, I didn't say that, I said . . .

Patient   . . . that you'd met a bear . . .

Doctor   . . . riding a bicycle.

Patient   Riding a bicycle, yes, it's quite common, riding a
bicycle.

Doctor   Please repeat after me: yesterday, I met a bear who was riding a bicycle.

Patient   Yesterday, I met a bear who was riding a bicycle.

Doctor   Again.

Patient   Yesterday, I met a bear who was riding a bicycle.

Doctor   Again.

Patient   Yesterday, I met a bear who was riding a bicycle.

Doctor   There. It's in your head.

Patient   I'm the bear all right. Dumb.

Doctor   It's in your head now?

Patient   Dumb as a bear . . .

Doctor   You've got a good memory?

Patient   Very good. Very good indeed.

Doctor   When you read something, you remember what you've read?

Patient   Every word. Even after a very long while . . .

Doctor   What have you read recently?

Patient   Recently, I read there was this man riding a bicycle, I'm not sure it wasn't you, and there was a bear behind him trying to catch up. Someone told me, I heard this morning, there was a bear on his tail right there behind his back. Or else he was on the bicycle and as for the bear, well he did as best he could. That's how they followed one another, as far as the church next door. That's it, the bear got on the bicycle, I know bears can ride bicycles, and the doctor was forced to admit that a bear was riding a bicycle.

Doctor   How old are you?

Patient   23.

Doctor   23 years old. (*He takes a mirror and gives it to the* **Patient**.) If you please, take a look.

The **Patient** *is deeply troubled.*

Patient   What's happened to me, doctor? Why is my . . .

His agitation is so great that the **Doctor** *has to restrain him forcibly.*

Doctor   Easy . . . easy . . . There . . . Let's go and look at the sea.

The **Patient** *sits. The* **Doctor** *leaves to take his coat. When he returns, the* **Patient** *looks up in pleasure as though seeing him for the first time.*

Patient   Good morning.

Doctor   Let's go and look at the sea.

They walk quietly side by side.

Doctor   What day are we today?

Patient   I don't know.

Doctor   What month?

Patient   I don't know.

Doctor   What year?

Patient   1963.

Doctor   No, listen carefully. Try not to forget.
It's the 15th of October 1990.

Patient   Are you sure?

Doctor   Yes.

Patient   The 15th of October 1990.
You're quite sure?

They reach the sea. The **Patient** *looks in wonder at the waves, follows the flight of the gulls.*

That's exactly how I thought it'd be.

Suddenly his interest fades and he turns away. For a moment, he and the **Doctor** *retrace their steps in silence.*

Doctor   What day are we today?

Patient   Don't know.

Doctor   What month?

Patient   Don't know.

Doctor   What year?

Patient   1963.

Doctor   What did you think of the sea?

Patient   I've never seen it.

Doctor   Would you like to see the sea?

Patient   Yes, I'd like to very much.
It must be very beautiful.

Visual Agnosia

*Two **Patients** are watching a film of the sea on a television screen.*

Doctor   Now, tell me, gentlemen, what do you see on the screen?

Patient 1   I see wavy lines, light grey, and other ones, lower down, horizontal, parallel, and dark grey.

Doctor   And you?

Patient 2   I see white stripes which get wider and narrower all the time: dark blue, light blue and white.

Patient 1   There are white oscillations in the middle and more dark grey lines, a little darker this time, and, in between the oscillations, white spots moving all the time.

Doctor   So, what could they be?

Patient 1   Perhaps computer images.

Patient 2   I don't know, but there is a majestic feeling of harmony.

*On a signal from the **Doctor** we hear the sound of the sea. The* **Patients** *laugh in surprise.*

Patient 1   It's the sea.

Patient 2   It's the sea.

*The **Doctor** sits and holds up a glove.*

Doctor   What's this object? No, don't touch.

Patient 1   It's a large rectangle, grey, prolonged by five descending cylinders, of different sizes, one of which is shorter than the others and slightly on a diagonal.

Patient 2   A continuous red surface, which seems to have five excrescences.

Doctor   What is it?

Patient 1   I don't know.

Patient 2   A sort of receptacle.

Doctor   What does the receptacle contain?

Patient 2   It contains its contents.

Doctor   Like what?

Patient 2   It could be a purse.

Doctor   For coins?

Patient 2   Of different sizes, for instance.

Doctor   Take it!

The **First Patient** *takes it, turns it over in his hand, examines it. Then almost inadvertently his fingers slip into the glove.*

Patient 1   It's a glove!

Patient 2   Of course, a red glove.

Patient 1   Oh, red.

Coffee is brought in.

Doctor   Help yourselves.

Patient 2 *(approaches the table, sniffs)*   Oh, coffee!

Patient 1   Thank you.

Patient 2   Thank you.

They take their cups and drink.

Doctor   Let's go on. *(He holds up a rose.)* What's this?

Patient 2   It's red and green.

Doctor   And you?

Patient 1   I see a long stick, very thin, with triangles stuck on it. At one end, there's a round shape with circles one on the top of the other. They are convoluted.

Doctor   What is it?

Patient 1   I don't know.

Doctor   Take it.

The **First Patient** *takes the rose, pricks his finger on a thorn.*

Patient 1   It's a rose. I didn't recognize it.
And I used to love roses.

He holds it out to the **Second Patient** *who takes it cautiously and holds it to his nose.*

Patient 2   An early rose. Superb. What exquisite odour!

Doctor   Tell me, gentlemen, how would you go about recognizing one another?

Patient 1 (*to the* **Second Patient**)   I think I'd recognize you, because you're very tall and thin and dark. (*He turns to the* **Doctor**.) But with you it's much harder. I see a grey curve, perhaps hair, perhaps a cap, and then a large rectangle, tomorrow I wouldn't be able to recognize you.

Doctor   That's a pity!

Patient 1   Ah! The voice! Then I'd know who you are.

Patient 2   As for this gentleman, I certainly wouldn't recognize him. But if I saw him walking I'd know him at once, as everyone has a special music in the way he walks. I'm a professor of music and I conduct an orchestra. One day one of my students arrived late and I didn't recognize him. .

Student (*off-stage*)   Good morning.

Patient 2   I only knew who it was when I heard his voice and even better, tac tac tac, the music of his steps. Bit by bit, I could no longer distinguish one face from another and I even saw faces where there were no faces. On another occasion, I took the coat-stand for one of my students. I said to him, 'Come over here! What are you waiting for?' Not a word, not a sign of life. Of course it was a coat-stand.
At first everyone took my mistakes for jokes and I was the first to laugh. But the day I mistook my wife for my hat, she took me to see an eye doctor, who said, 'Professor, there's

nothing wrong with your eyes, you have a problem with the visual areas of your brain, you must see a neurologist.'

Patient 1   Who said it's visual agnosia.

Patient 2   Precisely.

Patient 1   It's the same for me. When I look at my wife, I see the shape of her face but it's filled with little grey lines. For me her face has no meaning any more. And her whole body is grey. I feel disgusted.

Patient 2   Do you like music? Music is my greatest joy. Music sends me to sleep, music wakes me. I have a music for washing, a music for dressing, a music for drinking my tea. A music for taking a walk. I have a music for everything. Everything is music.

My Mother's Arm

The **Patient** *has both arms under the sheets. The* **Doctor** *lifts out his right arm and shows it to him.*

Doctor   Whose arm is this?

Patient   It's mine.

Doctor (*taking out the left arm*)   And this one?

Patient   It's my mother's.

Doctor   How did it get here?

Patient   I don't know. She must have forgotten it when she left the hospital.

Doctor   How long has it been here?

Patient   Since the day I came. Feel it. (*He puts the* **Doctor**'s *hand on his arm.*) It's warmer than mine. It's strong. My mother was a washerwoman.

Doctor   So where's your left arm?

Patient   It's there.

Doctor   Where exactly?

Patient   There, under the sheet. It's strange, but that's how it is. Just imagine, finding your mother's arm in your bed.

Negligence 1

*Another **Patient**'s right arm is under the sheet. His left arm is on top. The **Doctor** puts his right hand next to the **Patient**'s left hand.*

Doctor   Take your left hand.

Patient (*indicates the **Doctor**'s hand*)   Here it is.

Doctor   Where's your wedding ring?

Patient   They took it off.

Doctor   And this watch?

Patient   They put it on.

Doctor   But this hand is lighter than the other.

Patient   As it's paralysed, that's how it is.

Doctor (*pinching his own hand*)   Did you feel anything?

Patient   Of course not. It's paralysed.

Doctor (*moving his own hand*)   Funny, then, that you can move it.

Patient   Ah, that's something I can't understand.
If this hand moves it can't be mine.

Doctor   So, where is your left hand?

Patient (*hesitates then taps the **Doctor**'s hand*)   Here.

*The **Doctor** puts his hand next to the **Patient**'s left hand, drawing both into the **Patient**'s field of vision.*

Doctor   In that case, you have ten fingers on this side.

Patient   I don't know. It's very strange.

Doctor   So you have two left hands?

Patient   I wonder why.

Negligence 2

A **Second Doctor** *leads the same* **Patient** *away.*

Doctor   Why are you in hospital?

Patient   Ah, here we go.
Know or don't know I can't tell. I'm where I am. Whoopee!
It's not right. I'm 59 and I fell out of bed, flat on my face.
Not to know where I am at my age. My head's like a plate of
porridge.

Doctor   Tell me what you see in the room.

Patient   A chair, another chair, a gentleman dressed in
white.

Doctor 2   That's all. Nothing else?

Patient   Some white paper on the floor.

Another **Doctor***, on his left, plays on a mouth organ.*

Doctor 2   Where's the music coming from?

Patient   From there. (*He points in the opposite direction, to the
right. The* **Second Doctor** *turns the* **Patient** *to the left and he
sees the other* **Doctor** *playing the mouth organ.*)
Ah the musician's over there. Those are his notes.

Doctor 2 (*putting himself behind the* **Patient***, on his left*)
Where am I?

Patient (*turns his chair a complete circle to the right and discovers the*
Doctor)   There you are, doctor!

Doctor 2   Good. (*He goes to the far side of the* **Patient***. Only a
small turn to the left is needed to find him.*)   And now. Where am I?

Patient (*still on his chair does another large circle, always to the
right. Seeing the* **Doctor***, he exclaims with a big smile*)   You are
there, doctor!

Doctor 2   Well done.

Patient   All is crystal clear. Whoopee!

Negligence 3

The **Doctor** *sits the* **Patient** *beside a large square table.*

Doctor   Good morning. You live in Paris?

Patient   Yes.

Doctor   So you know the place de la Concorde? We're going to make a little trip in your imagination. This is the place de la Concorde, and this is the big column in the middle. (*He points to the table.*) Imagine you are standing with your back to the river Seine. Are you there?

Patient   Yes.

Doctor   From this viewpoint, describe what you see.

Patient (*indicates what he sees, always with the right hand, always on the right*)   I can see the rue Royale, the Ministère de la Marine, the big church the Madeleine, the rue de Rivoli, the Tuileries Gardens and the Obelisk.

Doctor   Is that all?

Patient   Oh! . . . I forgot . . . In the Tuileries, there's the Jeu de Paume Museum and the Orangery.

Doctor   Good . . . I am going to turn the place de la Concorde right round. Now, still in your imagination, you cross the square. You can still see the Tuileries?

Patient   Yes, yes.

Doctor   Good, carry on walking. You are now on the opposite side with your back to the church. Turn round. You're there?

Patient   Yes.

Doctor   You can see all the square?

Patient   Yes.

Doctor   From where you are now, tell me what you see.

Patient (*again, only indicates what is on the right*)   The Obelisk, the Seine, the Champs Elysées. The avenue Gabriel. The American Embassy and the Hôtel Crillon.

Doctor   That's all? So where are the Tuileries? The Ministère de la Marine?

Patient   I can't see them any more.

Doctor   Thank you. Open your eyes.

*An **Attendant** brings a razor, a mirror, and spreads a thick coat of foam on the **Patient**'s face.*

Doctor   I asked them not to shave you this morning. Do you mind shaving yourself, and we will watch you on the screen.

Patient   Very well.

*A video camera is focused on the **Patient**. The **Doctors** watch the close-up of his face. The **Patient** very carefully shaves the right side of his face. When he has finished, his face is perfectly divided in two, the left side untouched and thick with cream. The **Patient** wipes the right side with a towel.*

Patient   There.

Doctor   Now take a good look at yourself in the mirror. You haven't forgotten anything?

Patient   No.

Doctor   Turn round. Look at the screen.

*On the screen, on the right of the image, the **Patient** now sees his face. Half of it is covered with shaving cream. He looks at it, turns back to the mirror, peers into it, then painfully looks back at the screen, seeing again his face covered in foam. He is deeply disturbed.*

Patient   Please stop. Stop that!

Doctor   Thank you. Don't be ashamed.
You'll see, in a month you'll be much better. Don't worry. I'll come by tomorrow.

*(The **Doctor** leaves, switching out the light. The **Patient** is now alone in the dark as though back in the ward. He finds his left leg and with all his strength tries to get rid of it, pulling, kicking with his other foot, attempting vainly to tear it off. He falls on the ground with a howl of terror. The **Doctors** hurry in to help him, and as they lift him he cries out . . .*

Patient   Why have they put an amputated leg in my bed?

Loss of Proprioception

The **Patient** *is lying flat on his back.*

Patient   I've lost all the sensation of my body. My head moves, but from my neck to my feet I can't feel my body any more. If I don't look at it, I don't know it's there, it's as though it doesn't exist. The doctors explain to me that I'm not paralysed. They say I've lost my proprioception:

> Turned every two hours like a piece of meat
> Bathed with lotion
> Unmoving like a statue
> Mind filled with emotion
> Limbs dead to the touch
> Movement impossible
> Lying on a bed
> Eyes fixed on the flaking ceiling
> Wishing those flakes would turn to cracks
> And the ceiling fall
> To take me from that misery
> What's the use of an active brain
> Without mobility?

The **Patient** *now moves slightly and discovers his body.*

I've found out that if I look at my arm I can guide it with my eyes. Only my eyes can help me. I must use them to direct my hand towards the sheet, I take hold of it by closing my fingers, I can't feel anything, so I try to calculate the pressure it needs, and I pull it off to free my legs. Now my feet, I must put them on the floor controlling the movements with my eyes. I have made up my mind. I'm going to stand up. I must get my chest to tip forward, so I have to bend my head and swing my body. The only sensation I have is a tightening in my stomach. I mustn't close my eyes. I must watch what I'm doing, all the time. The tiniest distraction – and everything crumbles.

He struggles to his feet, while from behind the **Doctor** *watches him attentively. The* **Patient** *slowly walks forward.*

Now that I've managed to stand up, I can walk, but I can't turn round.

The **Doctor** *turns him.*

Patient   If I want to keep on my feet, I have to focus on a point on the wall to know that I am upright – even now when I am talking to you. And I can't do two things at once. I can stand and hold something in my hand, but if I want to walk I'm forced to look at my legs . . .

He takes a few steps and at once he crushes the paper cup the **Doctor** *has put in his hand.*

The doctors say, 'Neurologically, no progress.' Or else, 'You've learned to walk. Bravo!' They're right. Nothing has been achieved. I can walk today, but there's no guarantee I can do so tomorrow. Every day is a mental marathon. Nothing gets recorded, there are no habits, I've only tricks and strategies. I even learned gestures to let people think I am normal.

He sits back in his chair, crossing his legs. Then he gets up again.

Once, just once, when I was walking in the forest, I was able to look around me, listen, think and even dream. It only lasted for a few seconds, but it was marvellous to remember what it was like to be free.

Ticker

Ticker   I don't remember doing any of that. All those
ticks, hundreds of them, one after another. It's amazing. A
second before the tick I can see what's going to happen –
and I know why. I can see it in my face. I can see the
thoughts coming into my brain. I'm like a clock, the minutes
go by and you can't stop them, tick, tock, I'm carried away.
For instance, my nose. I can see my nose. My nose catches
my eye. The next second I turn this into a game. I look at it
from one side, from the other, I put on my glasses, get them
straight, see over the top, underneath . . .
When I take Haldol – we'll talk about that later – I get an
ache in my neck and right away I toss the pain over the
other side . . . Imagine doing this a hundred times a day, it
hurts . . . Are you filming? 'The Ticker's Tragedy. Part 2'.

He nips the microphone.

I know I shouldn't touch it, you said 'DON'T TOUCH
THE MIKE' but I can't help it. I love it. It's stronger than I
am. It's compulsive, like the need to bark or shout strange
words. I see myself as though I'm cut in two. One me ticks
all the time, while the other me says to him, 'Stop.' No, no,
steady, you're out of your mind, it's ridiculous, idiotic, I said
'Halt!' 'Verboten!'
I'm in a cinema watching a film about the deep South.
Suddenly I start throwing my hands in the air, shouting
'Alleluia!' The people in the cinema get angry but the more
they get angry the more the hands go in the air. The blind
force of the sub-cortex always wins in the end. A ticker
friend said to me the other day, 'I can never go to an
auction' . . . You know there are all kinds of tickers, tickers
who have no control at all and for them there's no way out,
no possible help . . . and then there are others who can
manage with a great effort to pull themselves together for a
moment and concentrate – I know a man, in Toronto, he
works for a big company, he's got an odd job for a ticker,
he's Welfare Officer. He sees people all day long, you'd

think he's very much together, all of a piece, 'Yes, oh yes,
yes, yes, madam, we will certainly see to it that there are no
repetitions of the problem in the future . . .'
After a time, he just can't keep it up any longer, so he says,
'Excuse me, madam, I'll be back in a moment.' He gets up,
locks himself in the gentlemen's toilet and then, 'Fuck! Fuck!
Fuck you! . . .'
He comes back and says, 'Yes, madam . . . as I was saying
before being called to the phone . . .'

Doctor   What about when you dream?

Ticker   In my dreams, I'm at peace, I do everything
normally and in the morning it's the same thing. I lie in bed,
I'm quiet, thinking pleasant thoughts and I laugh out loud
remembering the ticks I did the day before.
And when I play ping-pong, then I never tick, and if I
dance, it's my natural tempo, the tempo of my
temperament.

Doctor   Why can't you be like that all the time?

Ticker   Ah, that's a question we should ask you, Dr Sacks.
It's an enigma. You know why we are called 'Tourettes'?

Doctor   No.

Ticker   At the end of the last century there was a great
physician who worked in the Salpêtrière Hospital in Paris.
His name was George Gilles de la Tourette. One day, just
like any other day, he came down from the wards – of
course he didn't tick – and in the courtyard he ran into a
peculiar individual who greeted him like this . . . so the
doctor bowed, he bowed, bowed, bowed all the time, then
he began to bark, he said, 'Crisficks, cock-in-shit, thumb-in-
cunt . . . Satan – Satan!'
The doctor said to himself, 'What's forcing him to do that,
it's not the devil, it must be in the brain.' And he discovered
the syndrome. It was named after him the Tourette's
syndrome. It's in the thalamus, the hypothalamus, deep in
the brain, in the limbic system, the primitive zones of the

head where the feeling and instinctive factors of the
personality are buried.

Doctor   Quite right.

Ticker   There's a link missing between the mind and the
body, between the me and the it, between soul and body, a
link missing. That's me, isn't it?

Doctor   Yes.

Ticker   I've a tumour of the mind. Tumour of the Mind,
a thunderstorm in the brain, the electricity boils up,
suddenly explodes and for instance if a ticket collector just
looks at me and says, 'Ticket please', it's too much, I could
kill him. Or two people talk to me at once . . . But I can be
helped in my affliction by the medicine you gave me.

Doctor   Haldol.

Ticker   That's it. How are you, Haldol? I'm fine. When I
take Haldol I'm like this . . . And if I play ping-pong . . . I'm
like this . . .
You ticked, Dr Sacks, I saw it in the corner of your eye. Get
it on film! I present to you Dr Sacks –

Doctor   Cut!

Ticker   No, don't cut, it's very important, I present to you
the famous Dr Sacks who visits wild animals in the cage,
he's not afraid to enter the menagerie, he doesn't stay all
day long behind a desk in a white gown, he comes to us, he
films us . . .
Joking apart, it's no joke to be like this, and it's a joke, it
doesn't make me laugh and it's a good laugh all the same.
Of course, there's no neat and tidy place for me on this
earth, I have to make one for myself. The hardest part is
trying to live with a woman, because the children would
most likely have the syndrome – it's genetic, or so they say –
and even when I'm with a girl . . . well, that's it . . .
Sometimes I wonder, why me? . . . And then . . . You've got
to learn to live with yourself, haven't you?

Some people say the mind doesn't exist, while others say,
careful, it's not so simple – in the old days they'd lock us up
with the loonies, but now we are in all the best books:
neurologists, psychologists, neuro-psychiatrists, professors of
Cognitive Studies, we're in fashion. No one wants to know
us but we are in fashion. Yes, everyone wants Tourettes.
You want Tourette's, take mine. You want it, you can have
it . . . Fuck you – fuck you.

Japanese Songs

The **Patient** *is in bed, asleep. Suddenly, he wakes.*

Patient   Impossible. Japanese songs in the middle of the
night! They're beautiful . . . I must have forgotten to turn off
my radio. It'll wake up all the other old people. No, it's not
the radio. It's strange. I know it's quiet here, yet I'm in an
ocean of noise. Why am I the only one to hear these songs?
I wonder if the radio isn't simply in my head. It's very
disturbing having music in the head. It comes and goes all
day long now, I can't understand what people are saying.
It's not easy to live like this. I must see a doctor. But what
sort of doctor? An ear specialist? No. If it was an ear
problem, I wouldn't be hearing Japanese songs. Anyway
I've forgotten them completely. All the same, I'm not mad.
Ah! Perhaps it's because of the stroke that I had a long time
ago.
I should see a neurologist.
I feel my mother's arms, I'm three years old. I can see my
mother. I am in her arms.
She sings . . .
I can also see my father, he says . . .
In my home I was loved, cuddled, caressed. When my
parents died, I wasn't yet five, I was all alone and they sent
me to my aunt in China. I didn't remember Japan any
more.
But now thanks to these songs in my head I feel my
childhood's coming back again.
No, no, I don't want to be cured.
I need these memories.
I need these songs.
The door of my past has opened, a door that was closed for
so long.

The **Doctor** *brings him a medication, murmuring . . .*

Doctor   Your pills. Some water.

The **Patient** *swallows them. He is very sad. The music fades away.*

Patient   The door of my past is closed.

The Dream

A **Patient** *is eating a sandwich. The* **Doctor** *enters.*

Doctor So you're awake now?

Patient Yes, apart from the dream.

Doctor What dream?

Patient The dream. I'm at home in my bed and I'm dreaming about being in hospital. I've nothing to worry about, because I know that all this is part of my dream.

Doctor Yes, but we see one another every day. What do you make of that? This morning, just like every morning you got up, and right now you're eating a sandwich. So you must be awake.

Patient No. Listen. I've a place of my own, my very own place, and I've the hospital. Between the two, there's the night. The passage from my home to the hospital takes place during the night. Now I've come out of the night, or, if you prefer, I've woken up, inside my dream. But as I dream I've been in hospital for a long time, it's quite normal.

Doctor Do you realize you had an accident?

He shows the **Patient** *a scan of his brain.*

This is your brain. Here is the injury.
How can you explain this?

Patient It's obvious. If I dream about being in hospital, I need a very good reason for being there.

Doctor Do you think you are able to use the whole of your memory at this moment?

Patient Fuck my memory! Sorry, in a dream, sorry, in a dream you don't bother about your memory.

Doctor So who am I?

Patient　You are a character in my dream. You're here, talking to me, entertaining me, but in reality you don't exist.

Doctor　What is reality?

Patient　Reality means that tomorrow, my tomorrow, I'll wake up and at last it'll all be over. It's beginning to go on for far too long, I'd like to be able to wake up.

Doctor　Do you think there's a way of waking you up?

Patient　Yes. I often think about it.
It'd be to go up there, high up, up onto the roof of the hospital and jump – that would wake me. Or else when I hit the ground, the shock would wake me. I know I can't hurt myself because at this moment I'm in my bed. That's all it would need to set off the sort of fear in my dream that could wake me. Because apart from myself, I don't know who could wake me. God, perhaps. I don't know.

Doctor　So God has a place in all this?

Patient　I'm wondering who could have a place and as I know it isn't you who could wake me, I'm looking everywhere. I don't say prayers or anything idiotic like that, but every night, I ask Him to let me go tomorrow . . .

Broca's Aphasia

A **Patient** *is listening to a cassette. A* **Second Patient** *is waiting. The* **Doctor** *enters.*

Doctor   Good afternoon.
Do you like this music? Do you know it?

Patient   Yes yes.

Doctor   What's the name of the composer?

Patient   Yes yes.

Doctor   And what about you? Do you know the composer's name?

Patient 2 *mumbles incomprehensibly.*

Doctor   What?

Patient 2 *writes the name of the composer on a paper.*

Doctor   Correct. Please read what you've just written.

Patient 2   . . .

Doctor   Take a seat. (*He turns to the* **First Patient**.) And you, can you read it?

Patient   Yes . . . Difficult.

Doctor   Erik Satie. Can you see the words in your head?

Patient   Yes yes.

Doctor   And the letters? Can you see them?

Patient   Yes . . .

Doctor   For instance, the letter A. Show me the letter A . . .

The **Patient** *makes vague, unsuccessful attempts to draw an A with his finger.*

Patient   Yes . . .

Doctor   Have you ever seen the Eiffel Tower?

Patient   Yes . . .

Doctor   Show it to me.

Patient   Yes.

He draws in the air a perfect A.

Doctor   You've done a perfect A.
And the letter O? Show it to me.

Patient   Yes yes.

He searches vainly with his fingers.

Doctor   Show me a moon.

Patient   Yes.

He draws a perfect circle in the air.

Doctor   Now do a moon with your mouth and say 'O, O, O'.

*The **Patient** tries desperately, but in the end gives up.*

Doctor   Listen – today, we're going to say NO.

Patient   Yes.

Doctor   Say NO.

Patient   Difficult.

Doctor   You can say 'difficult', so now you can say NO.
Say NO, NO, NO . . .

*He suddenly stabs at the **Patient** with his pen. The **Patient** cries out.*

Patient   NO!

Doctor   Very well, you see, you've said 'no'.

Patient   Yes.

Doctor   From now on, you'll be able to say 'no'. Say NO, NO, NO.

Patient   Yes.

Doctor   That's enough for today. (*He takes out the cassette.*) You like this music, I'll give it to you.

Patient   Yes.

Doctor   Come back tomorrow.

Patient   Yes.

Doctor (*turns to the* **Second Patient**)   And you too, come back tomorrow.

Jargon

*The **Doctor** turns to another **Patient** who has been waiting patiently.*

Doctor   You haven't the same problem as the others? You've no difficulty in speaking now?

Patient   No none. There were moments it's true – you've found it – moments when I was well raised and rest. Rest. There we are, doctor, there we are. I was less inzest but reedy to want to do in good time. But noway to do it because illcommoded, pity, I'm completely nor. I haven't narrd nothing new extraordinary I can remain nothing in a clear precise way – too long perhaps – it's the thought that something comes – I come from a load, no, mowd the long road – I can do but I haven't found nothing good – nothing very good – nothing very very very well done – what – it's a pity – I must say spite of everything – I must be nawd; OK fine next scene?
You have already tringulated – dragged – incommoded – me – a first time – when your the ill of those contrary as well you have such treatment and there during these observenances – moating – not finding – not being – completing – some being nor voting – quite the reverse.
It hadn't been chapped – how do you say, owisay, in a newt way, newt the way you showed this wreckage – you didn't show that completely perfectly right – no? – it was profit – correct? – but we can rigidister it do you want? right – forced to hide it – that's all for now doctor sir madam that's all.

Doctor   Please sit down. Tell me, do you feel better now?

Patient   I was happy to have possibility to be fewer to do it – I was creded, but I was far from being able to credent you, to show you a bit of the verdigris, verdigris of something raw and mimigood, lumified, that's what you wanted – lumify to see something – that's it – so as to let it bounce, let it bounce, very very very good even if I prefaned

you the moment – pity – but I had moments – I remember
marvellously well – I had even goodness – very wishes – I
wanted to count black sharp photos snapped which wanted
to see new born new in – how can I say – I – in my good
forms and in my good everwises, what a shame – soligame
tame.

Doctor   Soligame tame?

Patient   Yes, I sleep. And I sleep a bit. And I sleep. Mott.
I mott. I'm a bit mogue. That's right. You've found it.

Doctor   Chaddergrame sinaway.

Patient   Exactly. That's exactly right indeed.
We've seen things being blundled, very blundled, that's it,
blundled, badly bominally not blinzied but plecise.

Doctor   Saberot Betamay.

Patient   Your ragger was tard of wanting to come to see
still something more, God's truth.

Doctor   Tell me do you like reading?

Patient   Ah, what rollish! Ah, very good, very reading
who wants to read ah 'in vitre meledis'.

Doctor   Then read me Gray's 'Elegy'. (*He hands the*
Patient *a book.*)

Patient   Oh, well done, doctor, well done.

He reads. Meanwhile, the **Doctor** *quietly starts a tape recorder.*

Patient   The vain midge in the line – I like that – good
gives pain to the time very good the bold the bold are old
are old old in the land's enfassfassekadie that fluorescence
like a mozer a mizerleen montin proling alin like asslin in in
cherchalinsirline – it's very, very fine salteen screen between
between of between tackatack.
This mantrangally crome from its montardly mite that
magropes to the mount – I've known that, it's good, very
good – millimay very good millimay chinasis. Comma, new

line. Machichain an na chain of the charn of the mageen
tike the less tutuspike and the tintispike was tintispoke and
the tintispoke was to tantifoke – since woweight the wodose
to waits then at braitenait from bry to bro soft flyflygank
there loozioubank of insinciane of insinciance oh! Sin sin.
I would be very glad to be born there thank you doctor.

Doctor   Listen.

*The **Doctor** rewinds the tape. The **Patient** hears for the first time
his jargon. For a moment this in unendurable and he cries.*

Patient   Ah, we're going there, ah, we're going to, we're
owing to . . .

Doctor   Don't worry it doesn't matter.

*The **Patient** recovers and listens with pleasure.*

Patient   Ah, well done, eh ah! . . . that's really good! Ah,
he had wine in the stills in a quick neat very beautiful, yes,
yes, a little furred, there – (*He cries again.*) Very good! Ah!
Oh! Very good. It's very good, doctor, it's a good likeness.
Countrified. Forgive me, stupid, swore a bit, I have wrong,
more, what for, idiotic, stupid.

Doctor   It doesn't matter. Don't worry.

Patient   It's grab. It's brear. It's numb. It's not, but it's a
pity. Give me back the button.

Doctor   It doesn't matter. We'll do something else.

*He lays a series of objects in front of the **Patient**.*

Now we'll do something else.
Please take a look.

Patient   What do you want again? Do you want to make
a new what? What? I would like the mountain. No, I prefer
contrary the mountain to the meter.

Doctor   Please give me the comb.

Patient   What which is it?

Doctor   The comb.

Patient   Yes no which do you want me to begin?

Doctor   I've already told you. The comb.

*The **Patient** is unable to identify it.*

Patient   For wool if a good thank you here.

Doctor   Give me the corkscrew.

*The **Patient** immediately recognizes the corkscrew, picking it up with pleasure.*

Patient   Chardonnay I would be deligh . . . be my – The Veuve Cloquot, good: vontage . . . we'd like to have it . . . but there is not . . .

Doctor   Good. Now, give me the key.

Patient   The key, it isn't.

Doctor   Look.

Patient   It isn't, it hasn't, we haven't so perhaps that too we can also have, same period. Ça, va, ça, va, n'est-ce pas?

Doctor   Give me the comb!

Patient   What that you've seen – finished – the comb – also – it's lost its detonator – such umberievable terrible – no! Absolutely not – too much – no!

He gets up angrily and makes to leave.

Doctor   Don't go!

Patient   Believe me we have finished, dear man – dear man – what you're doing all beauty – what you drag you finish it's too much.
With beauty – kind summer this time and finish and then nothing – you your goodness predicts your own – but we can't braid any more – correct. No you give very kindly you want nownet you want newsic – something which you growth. But you've no necessity to make beauty – you've no

necessity to do – it's goodnot – it's dead – black it's not
more truth – what you were recruiting – what you can finish
something that will be good to do – to black – it's finished –
it's well done and yet God knows I would like a thingamer –
revolver – a crime – a bat – a bite – to end that –

Doctor   Please.

Patient   That's all – no – no more life – you – you have
very well you very good – and the other people – yes – but –
because I was I – I can't do it – I am too young too ancient
age – 72, 88 years that I am old now – badmade – by law –
I am scraped – botch.

Doctor   Please.

Patient   I am dead – do you see, life no more truth – at all
– at all – to fall in life earth duly gift of gift with all of
beauty's kindness to all things – absolutely not.

Blindsight

A **Patient** *is sitting on a chair with a fixed stare. He is blind.*

Doctor   We know you are blind since you were 12. But we believe your eyes are intact and that a small lesion in the brain prevents you receiving the images your eyes transmit. If you agree, we would like to make a little experiment. A series of luminous points will light up, one after the other. Can you try to indicate to us the source of the lights?

The **Patient** *does so perfectly.*

Doctor   You have perfectly indicated the source of the lights.
Did you see something?

Patient   No.

Doctor   Did you feel something?

Patient   Absolutely nothing.

Doctor   Now, we would like with your help to make a second experiment. We will put an object in front of you and you will try to take it.

He does so.

Doctor   The object is in front of you . . .

The **Patient** *grabs it without hesitation. The* **Doctor** *holds out an object of a different shape and size.*

Doctor   Once more: the object is in front of you.
A third time: the object is in front of you.

This time the **Patient** *finds the object.*

Doctor   And now for the last time: the object is in front of you.

The **Doctor** *doesn't move. There is no object. The* **Patient** *searches vainly, pained and confused.*

Doctor   Let me reassure you. There was nothing.

Lightning Source UK Ltd.
Milton Keynes UK
UKOW030520150312

189011UK00002B/5/P